MY NAME IS …

First published in 2020 by
The Dedalus Press
13 Moyclare Road
Baldoyle
Dublin D13 K1C2
Ireland

www.dedaluspress.com

ISBN 978 1 910251 79 9 (paperback)
ISBN 978 1 910251 80 5 (hardback)

Dedalus Press titles are available in Ireland
from Argosy Books (www.argosybooks.ie) and in the UK
from Inpress Books (www.inpressbooks.co.uk)

Cover design: Pat Boran

Printed in Dublin, Ireland by Print Dynamics.

The Dedalus Press receives financial assistance from
The Arts Council / An Chomhairle Ealaíon.

MY NAME IS …

POLINA COSGRAVE

DEDALUS PRESS

ACKNOWLEDGEMENTS & THANKS

Acknowledgements are due to the editors and publishers of the following where a number of these poems, or earlier versions of them, originally appeared: *Writing Home: The 'New Irish' Poets* (Dedalus Press, 2019), *The Irish Times, Arena* on RTÉ Radio 1, NUI Galway Digital Collections, *Shamrock Haiku Journal* and *Qutub Minar Review.*

I would like to express my sincere gratitude to Pat Boran and Raffaela Tranchino at Dedalus Press for putting my work on the map of Irish writing and for promoting poetry in these insane times. Your professionalism and generosity are unparalleled. I would particularly like to thank Pat Boran for making me feel confident in my abilities and guiding me positively through the drafts. Without your continued support and encouragement this book wouldn't exist.

So many thanks to my fellow poets from *Writing Home:* Chandrika Narayanan-Mohan and Evgeny Shtorn for their friendship and help during the darkest hours of the lockdown. Much appreciation to the very talented June Caldwell for conversations that were vital in inspiring me to go on. I'm grateful to Anatoly Kudryavitsky and Mark Granier, whose insight and knowledge allowed me into writing poetry in English.

Gratitude in abundance to my parents for putting up with all my nonsense, you are my greatest treasure. Thanks to my Irish clan for welcoming me with arms wide open, to my Russian family for always having my back and to my Armenian gang for being such a blast. With love to my grandmother Zoya, who taught me to read and write at four *(Ба, я люблю тебя!)* and to my 8-month-old daughter Erika for sleeping uninterruptedly for an hour and letting me finish the acknowledgements: *Is breá liom tú.*

To my much loved stepson Aaron: this is why you need to read. To Jay: thank you for all the cups of tea you made me.

Special thanks to VN, who leads by example.

In loving memory of
Vladimir Gazaryan and Nikolay Reprintsev

Contents

an addition
to my coffee:
two spoonfuls of rain

A Summer Still Ahead

When the clouds were too close
And our lips too bright
Or vice versa
The nearest thing to romance known to men
Was to bring women roses
Stuffed in the flies of their trousers
Air was crisp and tense with wonder
We would chose to ignore
The time of day
So we could have breakfast
At midnight
With our eyes closed
When the words meant too much
And our wallets were thin
My only idea of a future was
The loaded gun of your breath
At the back of my neck
And a summer still ahead

My People

My people love to eat
the black apples of victory.
They fall from tall bony trees
like bombs in the night
leaving cracks in the yellow soil.
They lie around, these juicy mines.
That's when my people crawl on their bellies
to gather them into their helmets.
Filled with blood, ashes and gunpowder,
black apples explode in our mouths
like fireworks on Victory Day
tearing our intestines to shreds.
So we march with pride for
our city
our war
our dead.
My people dig up another hundred unknown soldiers.
We will never run out of them.
As long as we have our apple trees
planted by the victors
we will dig to find the inflamed roots.
Each time I eat a black apple
I smile like I still have a head.

No one left to love

He is so busy
smoking,
loving,
writing,
that he forgets what Putin looks like.
One day he wakes
on a planet
full of people
who talk like they matter,
who walk like they matter,
who sound like they really think they do matter,
and there is no one left to love,
nothing left to write about.
He packs his precious herbs
and moves to Saturn.

Starship

The blackest of holes,
the hottest of suns,
the craziest captain alive.
Surrender to none,
be gentle to some,
stay tough as the skies collide.
The milkiest way is over my head.
They're chasing me mile after mile.
This starship is mine,
try and catch me, I said.
This marvellous starship is mine.

Self-portrait

I'm almost young and comparably civil
for someone who nurtures her inner cynic,
I have a soft spot for Charles Simic,
Nintendo and soda bread.

I'm somewhat Russian and kind of solid
for someone who never knows when to call it,
I once loved a redhead, I wrote her sonnets,
but now the romance is dead.

She wished I had stayed in the capital city,
took care of her kitty, who's bald and unpretty,
She said I was deadly at cooking and *twitting*.
my words and my soup turned sour.

I wished she had moved with me to the Ocean,
but she couldn't swim, and I hadn't a notion.
We blew our life jackets out of proportion
and labelled each other as cowards.

It's crazy how even the Arctic winter
seems warmer than feelings which soon will wither.
I could live without her, but hardly with her.
It's not the winning that counts.

I'm lucky the sun in my garden is blazing,
I'm planting my saplings and I will raise them
with leaves full of poison and sharp as razors,
with crowns that shall pierce the clouds.

My Name Is

The name of an old man whose head was torn off by a bomb and
    whose body was left on the frozen soil of Stalingrad,
The name of his wife whose body slowly melted in times
    of hunger and cold,
The name of their daughter who carried her wounded child
    through the burning streets,
The name of her husband, who was imprisoned by the country
    he fought for,
The name of their little girl who survived the war and named me,
The name of a little boy that came to rebuild the ruins of the city
    with one piece of bread in his pocket, which was stolen by a dog,
The name of their son who once bought me a bullfinch in a cage
    so I could set the bird free,
The name of his great-grandfather who escaped from Nazi camp
    and got into a Soviet one as a punishment for cooperation
    with the enemy,
The names of four Armenian siblings who lost their parents
    to typhus and moved to the devastated Russia to establish a
    new generation,
The name of their father who had his name engraved on
    a Nagant revolver,
The name of his wife, Siranush, which means love, the
    only name that should be given to a woman,
The name of her great-granddaughter, who is the only reason
    I'm still here,
The name of her younger brother, who's been tortured in
    the pre-trial detention for six months and the name of what's
    left of him afterwards,
The name of his cousin, who's been beaten in the army for
    six hours and the name of what's left of him afterwards,
The name of my cousin, whose heart stopped on New Year's Eve,

The name of my grandfather, whose heart stopped when I
touched the Western Wall,
The name of his niece, whose cancer was as blistering as
    her passion for life,
The name of her nephew, who got a bullet in his head because he
    was Azerbaijani,
The name of my friend, who never woke up after her
    19th birthday,
The name of my friend, who never woke up after her boyfriend
    threw her out of the window on International Women's Day,
The name of my friend who never woke up after taking a pill,
The name of my lover, whose mind is murdered with drugs and
    depression, who goes into a war against his own madness
    each time he wakes up,
The name of the Unknown Soldier, on whose bones
    my hometown is built.
I am so full of names.
My name is a verb,
My name is to awake,
My name is to destroy,
My name is *cavt tanem,*
'I would take away your pain',
Say it like it's yours.

Say Yes

I love you in the mornings, as sunlight passes through clouds making them shine from the inside. I want to marry the lemon colour of your sky. You're full of gold, Ireland. Say Yes.

I love you when you're sad and grumpy, and I can hear the rain playing war drums on the roof and the wind is about to knock down the walls. You're full of power, Ireland. Say Yes.

I love you when you're cold as stone, when you teach me how to warm the room with my voice. I love you when you sparkle with laughter, when you remind me that seriousness kills poetry.

Nobody ever talked to me the way you do, Ireland. I love what you did to the English language, for in your mouth it is the language of humour and seduction.

I know you've been through a lot, and I have come to tell you you're beautiful and the best is yet to come. I promise to be true to you in good times and in bad. You are my perfect mirror that shows I can be so much more. You're full of life, Ireland. Say Yes.

Suitcases

If there was just one word for home
what would it be?
Is it where
or when?
Is home
your child's name?
That dish your grandma used to cook on Sundays?
The street you were born on?
The game you played with your schoolmates?
That song you danced to at your debs?
Your favourite pub?
Or rather
the swearing in the forsaken language
you can't help uttering each time
you stub your toe on a bed post?
Is that the closest you can get?
Or is it the smells and sounds and views
you sometimes dream of,
those things there are no new words for?

If so, what is the furthest word from it?
The least relevant word.
State? Government? The president's surname?
Maybe that empty feeling in your stomach
after you lost who you are?
Is it still there?

Is it the legacy hidden under your skin?
Is it the ache in your chest
caused by a long forgotten tune?
Is it the phantom pain of the roots you left behind?

Did you bring it with you
or bury it in your old garden?
Did you put it on the wall for everyone to see
or lock it in your suitcase?
That one word, too intimate, too yours to say aloud.
Too big to fit in any suitcase in the world.

Every Immigrant's Dream

Home is wherever your pet likes to sleep,
wherever your key fits the lock.
Pain only comes in the night
when you see what might have been
and wake up to find it's not real.
Mother tongue is no longer a tool,
but a treasure you keep to yourself.
The past is a hole in the chest
welcoming any breeze.
Isn't that every immigrant's dream?
all places reinvented,
all scars hidden,
all debts paid.

Surnames

I'm a Russian girl with an Irish surname,
who was a Russian girl with a Jewish surname,
who was a Russian girl with a Russian surname
who once spent nine months in a belly of
an Armenian girl with a Russian surname.
All these surnames
I can neither acknowledge nor return,
each opening or eclipsing the other
like a Russian doll.

Sad Mammals

Your call comes
from underneath a long night veil
draped over a different meridian.
Whoever you think you are now,
nurse me with your voice.
In this summer café
every person has another
except for me.
That woman is reading about breastfeeding,
those tourists are sharing meals and selfies.
I want to tell them I'm not an alien.
Nobody is.
We're all just scattered pieces
of one photograph,
sad mammals
breastfed by different mothers
with the same milk.
Think of the motley horses
running up and down
in the carousel:
they have no way out.
They comprise a perfect circle,
a single whole divided by their colours,
united by their motion.

What You Call Your Nose

Volgograd smells like T-34, lilac and lace,
Saint Petersburg smells like granite and grace,
Moscow smells like red flowers, gold and cement,
Dublin smells like blood and salt,
as for me, I smell of letters never sent,
as for you, you smell of stories never told.

Dog I Can't Keep

First language is a dog I can't keep anymore
barking in the back of my mind.
Stay, I command.
But it goes wherever it pleases,
reminding me who is the real owner here.
Its growling is so powerful that all other sounds get lost in it.
Your bites leave no scars anymore, I say.
I'll find you a new home, I say.
It grins.
First find yourself one.
Its jaws are closing around my neck.

Limbo

I am the distance
from the first cry to the last shit.
Neither former, nor latter,
but the void in between
refusing to be filled with certainty.
My head is a boiling pot
of languages,
Though my heart is at peace.
There are places I can hide
shapes I can take.
Anything to escape becoming someone.
Finality of choice is a burden for thought.
I like standing here watching the river flow.
I prefer twilight to any other time of day
for its possibilities. If I could be
a sentence, I would be a conditional one …
But no, you say, I'm wrong.
Twilight is just a period, what follows is inevitable.
Distances are to be traveled and choices will be made.
This river is about to reach the ocean.

And that one time

When my dad finally came home after a long trip and I was
    afraid I wouldn't recognise him,
When I saw my school sweetheart for the very first time,
When I knew I saw my school sweetheart for the very last time,
When my black cat passed away,
When I tasted cloudberry jam,
When they had to bury my friend before sunset due to the
    Muslim tradition and I couldn't stop staring at her young
    face,
When my colleague gave me a call in the middle of the night to
    say she was going to have a baby,
When I heard that carefree tune while waiting to sign my
    divorce papers,
When I got out of the house during a storm and accidentally
    met myself,
When I witnessed cherry blossom in the library garden in
    January,
And the city lights from above.

Sign

As a big orange of twilight
shattered the sky above us
into a dozen glassy clouds
each returning the warmth into our eyes
we're just standing there not blinking not breathing
afraid to miss
the last glare of sun reflected on silver roofs
beams jumping off mint green tank guns
on the marble pedestals
dappled light on the shoulders
of stone soldiers
there was a time when I thought
there's nothing much going in this city
"Please don't walk through the mass grave"
Life is never lost
It always returns to where it belongs
even if you're not part of it anymore

Insomnia Map

Insomnia is a train going nowhere.
Stuck in a loop
like that Whitney Houston song in my head.
When is my stop, I wonder.
I've seen this landscape many times before:
here's the valley of childhood memories,
where my grandfather gives me a wooden rifle
to make me the coolest kid in the neighborhood;
this is the river of self-pity,
where I drink rum and tango with the dead;
Let us go, you dummy, they whisper;
the desert of abandoned motherland,
where I can speak to ghosts,
who would shake their heads in disapproval.

And my favorite,
the street of no return,
where you walked me home from work last time
and we sat for hours under my window
petting a stray German Shepherd.
Another night,
another full circle.
Whitney wants to dance with somebody.
You must be lost, hun, I say.

Not as much as you.

Tattoo

Homeland
is tattooed on my skin,
and the picture is changing in real time.
Here is my school friend's fresh grave,
here is yesterday's theatre student
in a prison transport vehicle,
here are the ashes of Siberian forests,
here are the history books being rewritten.
And here is the apple tree in my parents' garden
blossoming, just like any other year,
and it's my favorite part of the tattoo.
One day I'll have the rest of it removed.

The Absence

I am the absence,
the light that left the kitchen
when candles were blown out,
the empty plate you had your beefsteak on,
your mouth right after
her lips escaped your lips.
I've lost my voice
and that's my voice now.
That much I know.
The price I had to pay
to disappear from any living space
was getting out of my own skin
and out of town for good,
the town that overfed me
with love and rust and cemetery soil.
I am the absence of that town,
the town that made me
from stolen air and awkward guitar tunes.
I saw you in my dreams
whistling those tunes
walking the streets of that town
wrapped in my skin.

Does *Alien* have a heart?

The homeless folk of outer space
we want to hug your troubled face.
and yet you hold us in disdain,
you'd like to have us back in chains.

You would oblige us if you could
embrace the price of motherhood
and be of use to our commune,
residing on this exomoon.

Obedient to the laws of hive,
we know well how to live our life.
Meanwhile, they're nothing but a con,
those moral grounds you're standing on.

Our acid blood and primal scream
are pieces of your broken dream.
We're gorgeous things beyond repair,
like Giger falling down the stairs.

H.R. Giger was a Swiss painter best known for his design work on the film Alien. He died after having suffered injuries in a fall on stairs.

Culture

Culture is your enemy.
A growling beast, it scratches your wounds
and feeds on your dreams.
Look it in the eye.
It's so easy to dissolve in the sea of noise.
Can you please switch off the culture?
Bombarding your mind with images of national pride,
brands you have to buy,
wars you need to fight,
and words you must say to fit in.
Switch it off, learn to be yourself.
Listen to the distant echo
of what used to be your song,
When you could still step out of line
and stop marching towards oblivion.
Listen to that melody, let it wake you up
to the magic of mankind,
to the power of no make-up,
to the bliss of being naked,
recall
you are Icarus,
you've chosen to fly high
because you have sunshine in your veins.
The fall will break you into a thousand golden pieces,
lighting the path for others.
recall
you are Voyager in interstellar space,
breathing starlight,
inhaling comets.
You'll never get home again
but you'll show us the rings of Saturn.

Switch off the culture,
and in the darkness of our hearts
we'll encounter each other for the first time
lit by nothing less than the bonfire of spirit.

One of you

Whoever made me
made my skin
from ash tree bark,
cut my body
from limestone,
filled my veins with river water,
my voice with prairie wind,
poured wheat beer into the systole,
lust into the diastole,
sealed my heart with poplar sap.
And whoever took me away
from the place of rest and desolation
and threw me into the pot full of people,
had the best intentions in mind —
to make me one of you,
to make you one of me.
But I broke your bones
with these metal hands
when I tried to hold you.
And you stole my face,
because you thought it could glow in the dark
as if in every wrinkle of my lips
there was a hidden star.
But there is not.

Four Walls

Four walls of silence
four walls of blindness
a young woman stuck
in the bulging stomach of a house
on every street
in every city
doors are closing behind their backs
like Venus flytraps
Another one got caught tonight
Slowly her skin becomes one with the wallpaper
Her eyes merge into the double-glazed windows
her right hand grows into the frying pan
her left into the vacuum cleaner
Is it a woman turning into the house
Or it is a house in the form of a human?
Blinking its curtains
breathing in draughts
Let's hope
her silhouette will blend in with its surroundings.

March

Summer night
crucified on a window frame
I've been lost for so long
I forgot my name
Would you set me aflame
Would you give me a spark
Don't you say we belong in the dark
Lights off
we pray for the sun to rise over our heads
counting stars in the boundless sky
marching through never-ending night
We will never stop
We will never hide
Born to fight
the dead inside
we shall stand our ground
and protect what's true
I can feel you're around
I believe in you
Don't betray our dreams
Liberate your mind
Give me light
Show me the pride of your tribe
Switch on
Remember what it's like to be alive
Let darkness fall
Our hearts will glow
with radiance
Our blood still flows

The Weapon

And the flame that keeps on searching
keeps on searching for the wick
and your smile when no one's watching
is a trick behind a trick
And the things forever sleeping
ever slipping from your hands
and the sunrise that you're skipping
is a silent reprimand
Ask for knowledge
Be a savage
It's the only choice you've got
It's a forage
without damage
Trust the weapon of your thought

Why do they fear poets?

Why do they fear poets?
Why do they want poets caged?
Blindfolded?
With hands tied and mouths shut?
Do poets steal? Or kill?
Is poetry corrupting?
Does it send our children to war?
Does it enslave?
What great power lies in poetry
that makes them terrified?
A poet in chains is still a poet.
words written in exile,
rhymes uttered in confinement
are even stronger.
Infinity can hear them better.
A poet's voice is made of steel.
A poet's mind is the sharpest sword.
Its echo will pierce through every wall
and reach people's hearts.
Why do they fear poets?
Maybe something like that.

He who unnamed me

I haven't said a word in a month. My tongue is rolled up, touching the hard palate. I'm not interested in speech anymore. I'm not a story to tell.

There are things on the table and no one to look at them. Yet, they are being observed. A laptop with a crack on its lid, a bitten chocolate bar, a silver coin heads-up. There is a keyboard drumming. *Dam di dam.* There is a hand approaching a head: pale fingers run through short straw hair. A sensation comes. There is pleasure. Between us there is a lasting viscous pleasure. It fills the air with raw sweetness and turns every gesture into slow motion fireworks. It is not being cared about.

We don't talk. He, who unnamed me, takes a deep breath and goes down to the kitchen to make his mint tea. The bells ring: he opens the door to let the cat in. He sits on the floor and chants. Mornings are always like that, except for the symbols appearing one after another on this screen. Typing feels like speaking. A voice can be heard.

The voice belongs to a figure I used to be when I had a name, when I was still fiction. I am here to register. I am. He, who unnamed me, gave music to these bones. It plays itself when our breaths get sullen. Nobody composed that, it has always been here.

I am the graveyard of his thoughts. I am not. You've forgotten to water the lilies, he indicates, whoever you are now.

What woke up

I remember the night I didn't survive and what woke up the
    morning after wasn't me anymore
I can remember that wet July night I didn't survive and what
    woke up the morning after was different
I think I can remember one night I didn't survive and how
    something woke up instead of me the morning after
And a kiss on my skin
Yes, that kiss which burned my thin pale neck
But the metal kiss is still burning on my neck, connecting the dots
So am I still the one that
Woke up instead of me?
Woke up dead instead of me
Woke up screaming instead of me
What woke up the morning after is slowly forgetting the night
    I didn't survive.

Bloody Soles

When another inside you dies
should you bury the words
they once wrote
about
the lovers
the traitors
the sunrise
about
the unrepeatable
as claimed by the corpse?
I do.

They're dangerous.
What if these words leave
a trace
with their bloody soles?
After cleaning up,
nobody wants red footprints
on a white carpet.

And yet,
we ought to honor them.
Let's put them on this person's grave,
words as flowers.

When another inside you dies
the words
they once wrote
still breathe
and laugh
and weep
and rage

And yet,
we'll have no mercy.
Let's bury them alive
faithful wives of an ancient king
after his battle is lost
after his body is brought home.

Room

They wake up nose to nose. She puts her hand on his chest and feels the pumping. His heart is beating like a war drum. She rips it out, takes it to her ear and listens to the rumble. As if it was a seashell. Meanwhile, he hears the stutter of a machine gun. Her thoughts are a string of bursts piercing his temples, they occupy all the space in the room. And the heartless boy plunges himself so deep into the girl she forgets to breathe.

Let's get out of this room. You don't want to be here when they detonate. The boy has already pulled out the pin. There will be blood boiling fire. Blinding fire reaching you through this keyhole.

Untwisting DNA

First lock my wrists
by gazing at the center
I hide behind a face
behind a face
behind a face

Don't let me move
until you notice
the thing I was
before I got this body

Then shut my eyes
by making it unbearable
to watch a force of nature
like you
whispering my name which I no longer need

Find a mirror in me
shallow
non-existing
without an image of you
waiting for your features to appear on its trembling surface
It's there to reflect your desires
to speak with your mouth

I'll follow you into the dark
untwisting my DNA
Free me from the tyranny
of the second-signal system
which uses me to make
sense of the world

Down down down the chain
from great apes to reptiles
this limbic cortex is nothing but
a bloody bell that goes ding-ding-dong
whenever it detects your presence in the room

Clumsy life on wobbling legs
all is wrong but you
Be the design in the chaos of a female's flesh
It loves no man
It's hungry for a god

Can I be white clay
wrapped in the lace of blue veins
submissive to your hands?
Can't you see I come alive
at your touch?

I will only feel
what you want me to feel
I will only believe
what you tell me to believe

Build me
formulate me
Call me into being
Recreate me as
a gracious dragon
at your service

Full of Swans

I couldn't move
in a room full of swans
in a body full of secrets
with your eyes on us
I couldn't breathe
Each bird
had a yellow ribbon on its webbed foot
in the pond of your mind
We were all bound
by one rope
I couldn't fly away
My feathers got wet
legs tangled
in your lying tongues
My heart sank while we dived
to the bottom of your delusion
Couldn't tell my skin
from yours
Weakness
never got me that far
As you put a leash
around my white neck
I wouldn't move

Like You

I want to sing like you,
so that when I open my mouth
cicadas would jump out of my head
and share their secrets,
So that when I reach a higher note
a wildflower would spring
from the ditch of my diaphragm
and grow all the way to the ceiling,

So that when I take another breath
coastal winds come to fill my lungs
with a new force. If I sang like you
would you listen like I do?

When you were gone

When you were gone
there was an unfinished chess game on the table
waiting for you to make the next move

When you were gone
I could still hear you favourite radio programme
playing Spanish guitar in the kitchen

When you were gone
your rocking chair was swaying as if you never left it

When you were gone
your books kept talking to me in your voice

When you were gone
the aroma of your coffee lingered in the room
like a gentle reminder to enjoy the day

I want to stay just like you, when I am gone.

Stasis

Green is the heart, I promise.
Don't bother digging in,
I swear, my heart is green.
You won't believe me, no.
Come on, then, grab a shovel,
and cut right here, I'll show you.
My heart is full of grass,
I swear by all the insects that hide inside my body,
by bugs and worms and tickling little ants.
They grow right through the heart
towards the sunshine,
those piercing blades of grass.
Green is the heart,
and grey the blood.
You won't believe me, no.
My blood is grey,
my flesh is stone and clay.
I swear it by the rains
and streams which fill my body,
those streams that lick my toes.
I am the land,
my mouth is full of soil,
so are the eyes and ears.
Wet is the breath.
warm is the voice, I promise.
My melting lungs
are glistening with dew.
The thighs are sweet, I swear.
I'll wait for you.
I'm waiting for you here.

Your Hands

Your hands built and built and built,
they've built memorials, hotels and universities,
they've built a city for me to live in.
A house for us to love in, a kitchen to laugh in, a table to sit at.
They've made rings for my little fingers,
they've made toys for my little hands,
they've made flutes for my little lips.
You told tales.
Tales of before war, tales of after war, never about.
And when you told tales your hands were building them up for
    me in the air, so that I could see. And I still do.
You would make a gesture of sticking a branch of a tree in the
    rich black soil of the place you came from.
'Just like that. And it will bloom,' you'd say.
'That's how good the land is to us.'
But the land of where you ended up wasn't so good, so your
    hands dug, dug and dug the dull soil of the prairie,
and they planted and planted and planted,
until they've made a garden full of berries and apples, a dozen
    kinds of apples,
so many different apples I had to give names to the trees they
    grew on.
Your hands planted and planted,
till they'd made a special garden for me,
till they'd made gardens for each of us.
Those hands, where did you get them?
Your father survived the concentration camp because he was a
    handy man. Did you get them from your father?
When I held your hand, was I holding his as well?
All the trees you've planted grow through me,
their roots kept standing when all I could do was crawl.

All the bricks you've laid kept me safe in whatever debris I found
  myself in.
I'm looking at my face in the mirror trying to trace your features.
I'm looking at my hands in the hope that they will do half as
  good as yours.

A Collection

Just like cards in the hand of a magician
poems appear out of thin air.
They arrive from nowhere
to use you as a pen
and your life as a notepad.
You don't force poems, but thank them
if they reveal themselves to you.
You ask them to come in
and if it's okay to write them down,
You ask them how far they'd like to go.
Some of them stay written on your heart,
because that's where they belong.
I am a collection of those
that fly back into the magician's hand
and merge into nothingness.

Good Omens

My granny once told me
a whirlwind of leaves and golden dust
in the early autumn
is nothing less
than the devil's wedding

My granny also mentioned
that if you manage to throw a knife
in the very heart of this whirlpool
you will see
the devil's black blood
dripping on the ground

So when I see somebody standing
in the middle of the street
with a knife covered in black blood
and it's late September
I know for sure: our grandmothers went to the same school

Favourite Word

Mangetsu. Full moon.
Your favourite Japanese word.
A round white magnet hanging
over Ueno Park,
where whales are swimming in the open sky,
where you can hear fox spirits creeping around,
if you listen carefully with your guts.
Just sit there, warm yourself
with the laughter of autumn leaves,
and watch a man smiling down at you from Mangetsu.
Take a deep breath
as if your lungs were two bags of unfinished letters
and exhale them for the wind to carry away.

About Water

Life is all
about water,
of water,
by water.
But do I know?
Do I speak its language?
A fish learns what the ocean is
only after it is pulled from the water.
I don't know my ocean, I don't know my life.

A fisherman pulls his net out of the sea,
breaking the dark surface, which reflects the sky.
not a net full of scales, but a net full of stars.
He knows his sea.

A little girl chases after a wave,
leaving footprints on the sand.
The wave agrees to play her game
and returns to shore almost at her heels.
She always wins, she knows her sea.

Me, I explain the sea to lovers.
I explain it to strangers.
Even to myself, I explain.
Then I touch the water, my hands
salty, my skin wrinkled.
Where do you end and I begin? I wonder.
The ocean replies: Really? That is what
you've come here to ask?

Heat

The kind of heat
That licks your skin off
with its scorching tongue
The kind
that cooks you alive in your own sweat
like a small fish on a rusty frying pan
But also
the kind of heat that weaves
sunbeams into your hair
turns salt glistening on your shoulders
into diamonds
That kind of heat
that found him
on a busy Friday
in late July
his 22nd year on Earth
when he came up with a song called "Snow"
because his eyes were melting away
his guitar caught fire
the strings charred
he opened yet another bottle
of doubt
a bottle he kept for days like these
and a pale girl poured from it
smelling of pepper and childhood
You're making things up again, she said
and he was. And he knew it well
But are they good things? Are they any good?
They're worth, admitted the girl
ever afterwards just a blister on his finger.

Satire

Donald Trump is not as orange as they say,
Not as orange as this sunset, that's for sure.
Though his hair is like a stack of hay,
still it lacks some countryside allure.

Greta Thunberg is not as loud as thunder,
not the one which makes our huskies howl,
Putin is not as deadly as the spider
crawling underneath my bathroom towel.

Zuckerberg is kind of omnipresent,
though not as much as mould inside the wardrobe,
Hillary is sharp as a lunar crescent,
but she's not bright enough to make your jaw drop.

Everybody thinks they have the power.
The natural way of things is quite dishonoured.
Orange is my very favourite colour.
Would you give it back to people, Donald?

Dublin is a Song

Dublin is a song
in a language spoken by lovers
muddled between the sheets.
It starts just a second before
they stop being human.
One keeps begging for more
of something the other never had,
but it's working out so well
they choke on madness
and the sound echoes in the hotel room
so bare: waves on a rocky shore,
wood crackling in a fireplace,
wind whistling through heather and thistle
every time their bodies meet.
This is what I heard on Talbot Street.

Dessert

What if you taste like winter sky?
What if you taste like 4 in the morning?
What if you taste exactly like my favorite song
if I ever had one?

What if I am bitter as a headache?
As a widow's breath?
As a cigarette butt in a bed of hyacinths?

I'll put you in the box with my stale bread
where no one will find you
and treasure you like my very last meal

I Told You with My Body

You already know,
I told you with my body.
I want to fight you in every way I can,
question everything you are:
from your eye colour
to the language you speak.
I want myself to drink from your speech,
erase the words you write
and explain
that there is no such thing as a personality.
You are as much as an entity
that feels like fire
and a home
at the same time,
But if I'm burning
how will I save my place from the flames?
But you already know,
I told you with my body.
You are new to me
in the way you wear your lips,
in the way you wear my lips.
Could you be real in the story of me?
Like death,
like drowning,
like a barfly,
like a lover,
like a listener,
like a passer-by,
like a foreigner,
like a memory imprinted between my thighs?
I want to learn
who you are

and after you change your skin
I'll be there to relearn it.
Then you can question everything I am.
How far will I go to get what I desire?
But we already know,
I said that with my body.
I would trade my dozen jobs
and all the men
I kept in my bed
and all the women who kept me wondering what I am made of
for watching the river flow
as you are breathing next to my shoulder.
Can I be real in the story of you?
Would I be more significant
If I disappeared
from web pages
immigration offices
people's minds?
Nobody matters.
However,
if you were all I knew about human beings
it would be enough.
I think I've already told you this with my body.

Plum and Cherry

A grafted tree showing different blossoms
plum and cherry petals dancing in the wind
sugary smell of lust
nauseating
a premonition of catastrophe
those meaty sweaty berries are going to come
Life is pouring dizziness out of a bottle with fresh spring
into my shattered glass
The only thing that lingers
is the air inside the bubbles
A grafted tree: two different blossoms
not ripe yet
Only a hint of future and youth
promise presence perspective potential
What is the right word for it?
A Plum branch connected to a cherry one
tree blood around the cut
Just like my English grows from my Russian roots
I hope it lives
I hope there will be fruit

First Poem

She is talking to me
from the womb, this girl
She is reading
in her native language
Language of darkness and warmth
She uses her own alphabet
watery symbols
bubbles of light
to create her first poem
I feel her
jab jab
cross
hook
uppercut
kick kick kick
in the uterus
sending signals to the organs
I hear her message
vibrating in the bones
in English it means:
wait till you see me
wait till you hear me
I bet you've never met
anyone like me

Free Dive

The pelvic bones are parting like the Red Sea on Moses' command.
I know her eyes are open wide in the dark, lashes touch as she
    blinks.
When she dreams, I wonder what she dreams about.
Does anything else exist for her other than this nine-month-long
    free dive in the amniotic fluid?
Maybe she sees herself as a pearl hunter
fearlessly exploring the depths?
She collects the treasure and, on just a single breath, surfaces
    from the ocean floor!
Or maybe she stays underwater a little longer to play with the
    sparkling fish?
To find a secret cave full of skeletons and pirate coins! There is
    something else, a note I left for her on the mossy wall:
Pain is a sign of life.
While the pelvic bones are parting like oyster shells to reveal the
    pearl,
My heart grows whole.

Lullaby

The tar-like darkness is all you've seen so far.
But time will come you'll know the touch of comets.
I'll pave your way with the jewellery of the tsars.
I promise.

My only peace is guarding at your bed.
My only purpose is to hear your laughter.
I am your soldier up until I'm dead.
And after.

You soon will break the prison of my bones,
the second heart in me is getting stronger.
You are the one to whom my first belongs.
The world is yours to conquer.

Metal Tide

My bedroom window faces a supermarket
and every morning I wake up
from the noise the trolleys make
when pushed into each other
It's the sound of waves crashing on the beach
a silver sound of freshness
I open the curtains to watch
the ocean of trolleys rise

Invisible Thread

As a child is chasing a kite down the shore line
her laughter lights up the empty beach
rhyming with the sun glare on the water
Your dream is connected to you by the same invisible thread
Don't let go